Ugly Baby

A Collection of Short Stories

Kathryn Rodrigues

With thanks to Deb, Mary and Brian.

Copyright © 2017 Written by Kathryn Rodrigues

All rights reserved. No part of this publication may be reproduced, distributed, or transmitted in any form or by any means, including photocopying, recording, or other electronic or mechanical methods, without the prior written permission of the publisher, except in the case of brief quotations embodied in critical reviews and certain other noncommercial uses permitted by copyright law. For permission requests, write to the publisher, addressed "Attention: Permissions Coordinator," at the following email address: uglybabybook@gmail.com

For Aunt

Contents

Kathryn Jean	7
An Average Day	9
Butt Out	11
Gibbs	13
Dolls	15
The Last Thanksgiving	17
Emily Alice	21
Elephant Show	23
My First 10 Speed	25
Iced Tea	27
The Night	31
Walking	35
Woods	37
Bob	39
Truffle	41
Landslide	45
Four for Four	47
Starbucks	49
White Rabbit	53
Cash	57

Missed Connection
Providence, RI

White Missy Elliott looking for a lost friend.

I saw a handful of people hanging out by the back of the Arts Center. When I noticed your tour bus, I knew I had to stick around. It was freezing, but thankfully, I had on my neon Adidas hoodie to keep me warm.

About 45 minutes in, after most of the other groupies had left, there you were. You stopped and made eye contact with me. I froze. I didn't know what to say or do. So, in a panic, I simply lifted my right hand and gave a tiny wave, all while smiling in the most terribly uncomfortable way. Then you said "I'm going inside. I'll come right back out."

I waited. And waited. You never came back. Was it the wave? The smile? The sweatshirt?

All I wanted to do is hang out and tell a few stories to you. So, Dave Chappelle, if you're reading this, get at me. I'm ready to try again.

Kathryn Jean

My mother, a chain smoking 31 year old, had suspicions she was pregnant. After getting her period, and having gained no significant weight, she blocked it out.

Must've been in her head.

Until the night of November 16th, 1982.

My aunt came downstairs to use the bathroom. She, my mother, my uncle and my grandfather all lived in a house together.

"Eileen. I need to use the bathroom. What's that sound?"

"A baby"

My aunt, to this day, tells me her first reaction was "what an ugly baby." She loves that part of the story.

So, my mother, had delivered a baby. By herself. Her only prenatal care found in her countless packs of Newports.
No one could believe it. Even when the rescue arrived, they made their usual course to my grandfather's room, only to be redirected.

So, that's how I came to be. A tiny, 4lb baby. Birthed in the shit house. Destined to be a weirdo extraordinaire from day one.

An Average Day

-Go to school event. Joke around in the hall and drop phone, breaking glass. Initial rage sets in. Say things out loud that most certainly shouldn't be said inside a school.

-While watching said event, run into an old friend from high school who points out that I have dropped a maxi pad on the cafeteria floor.

(You know, one of the ones in bright packaging. Can't miss it)

-Brief trip to Wal-Mart. That speaks for itself.

usual sleep pattern of waking up at 3am and contemplating life's bad decisions

-Get to court and walk through the metal detector with pockets full of papers, but with the paranoia level of someone who hiding a weapon in their asshole. -go upstairs and find the most inconspicuous perch. Then said "She crawls into your ear and rapes your brain. Your body is still there experiencing her, but your brain just took the 60 bus to Newport" to a state employee.

-Go to the Spanish market to get quality bread and snacks. Have awkward English/Spanish send-off interaction with cashier

several traffic situations where I'm not sure if I should go or they should go. Maximum awkwardness now mixed with anxiety

-Go to the dentist. Dental hygienist offers to hang my coat up in the back. I hear her wrong and go into a stuttering awkward story about how I don't know where to go. We stared at each other silently for a minute, then I give her my coat.

-Go to supermarket to grab a few more things. Stare blankly at cashier who feels I lack the proper "ethnicity" to purchase Caribbean produce.

That was from 7pm Tuesday until 3pm Wednesday.

Maximum awkwardness.
All day. Every day.
Can't stop. Won't stop.
Please send help.

Butt Out

Changa had snuck one litter in before we could take her to be fixed. She had a real tough time with the last kitten and wasn't acting herself. She had given birth to 4 healthy kittens, but wouldn't feed them. The next morning, we took her to the vet. Turns out she developed an infection in her uterus and would have to be on antibiotics. It also meant that now I would have to be the kitten mother. I was given proper instructions:

-Fill a sock with rice and microwave it. They will snuggle as they would their mother.
-Wake up every few hours and bottle feed them.
-And last, but not least, take a warm cotton ball and rub their crotch and ass after they eat so they can go to the bathroom.

What. The. Fuck.

Apparently, that's why mama cats do so much ass licking. The babies can't go to the bathroom unless they do.

Sick, I know.

Even sicker that I had to be the ass rubber. Just what I've always wanted.

Anyways, I did what I was supposed to for a few days and noticed one of the cat's ass looked swollen. I ignored it, figuring it would resolve itself.

Nope.

It just slowly slid out further and further until the other kittens, blind as shit, started sucking on it thinking it was a nipple.

I shit you not.

So now I have to take this tiny kitten to the vet to fix her ass. They tell me it's a prolapsed rectum. They'll put her ass back in and sew it shut, and I had to take her back the next day. If it stayed in, she'd be ok. If not, they had to put her to sleep.

Great news. It stayed in. And, after all that work I put in, I decided to keep her. And name her appropriately, Butt Out.

Gibbs

In July of 2000, I started the Katharine Gibbs School. $17,000 for a piece of paper that essentially says I was pretty good with font choices and graphic design 17 years ago. Part of my failure with that was because they were a sham school, and part was because I was unwilling to leave my womb of a small town.

While I was there, we went on a field trip to visit an artist at his Pawtucket studio. We walked in this old mill building that reeked of paint, one of my favorite smells. His studio was filled with all these massive, magnificent paintings. Our teacher obviously was good friends with the dude, they seemed pretty happy to see each other. She explained to us that his art had just been on display at some awards show. Grammys, Emmys... I can't remember which one. He talked for a little while, explaining his success and history. I can't remember any of those details either. I think I was just too consumed with my environment. He did catch my attention when he told us about his biggest fan, himself. He went on this tangent about how he loved himself. He loved his work. And how he should because if he didn't, how could he expect anyone else to? We left and the majority of my classmates went on and on about how the dude was such an asshole. Totally dismissing the magnitude of talent the guy had. That shit blew my mind, even at 17. Why? Why was he an asshole?

Because he didn't give a single shit about any of our opinions about his art? Because he was confident? They knew nothing about him, as a person. To be fair, neither did I, but to simply label someone an asshole because they don't fit your mold is a garbage way of thinking.

We need more assholes, the good kind.

I'm not talking about people who are mean just to be mean. Or people who are entitled and selfish because of their entitlement. Or people that hurt others just because they can. I'm talking about the truth tellers.

The people who don't sugar coat things in an effort to not pop your fragile bubbles. People who will call you out for being a dick. If you meet someone who is genuine, but their views don't match yours so you don't like them, that doesn't make them an asshole.

That makes you one.

Dolls

In the early 90's most kids my age were having slumber parties and trying not to murder their Tamagotchis. Me? Nope. I was going from shop to shop in pursuit of the latest porcelain doll with my mom and aunt. Once you're too big to hide in the center of shirt racks and convince your mother you've been abducted, going shopping with her sucks. Never mind being stuck in a 10×16 store filled with breakable shit for two hours. In retrospect, I guess it was good practice for having a MRI.

Now that I'm an adult, sort of, I think about those damn dolls. I've learned that not only were they insufferable because they, no doubt, were going to steal my soul while I slept, but those fuckers went for about $200 a kid. No joke. So I'm sitting here, 34 years old, thinking about the whole scenario. You know what pisses me off the most? My mother's garbage financial priorities? My robbed moments of precious youth? No. I am salty as shit that we could spend $200 on Baseball Baby Ricky, but those two couldn't buy me a motherfucking Ken doll. All my friends had Ken dolls. Some even had one Ken for every Barbie. Not me. I had a polygamist ranch, disguised as a dream house, run by

Stretch Armstrong, He-Man or whatever wrestling dude my cousin Pete wasn't using anymore. Absolute and complete bullshit.

The closest I ever got was Jordan from New Kids on the Block. You remember Jordan? He was the ugly, shitty one with the rat tail.

One day, the time will come for me to face those plastic containers filled with porcelain nightmares, and when it does, I'm ready. Ready to sell every fucking one on eBay.

And after I'm done spending that cash on my water bill and Hibachi, I'm gonna stop at Target and buy that damn Ken doll.

Watch out, Beanie Babies, you're next.

The Last Thanksgiving

When I moved out on my own, holiday dinners got moved to my apartment. I had my shit together more than Aunt, and all the other siblings either lived too far or were institutionalized. Not that either of my uncles would have been capable had they not been. They were good at weed and arguing. And arguing about weed. Not entertaining. I have memories from my childhood of looking out the three porch windows and seeing Uncle Johnny chasing Uncle Eddie with an axe. At my late Aunt Sue's funeral dinner, they sat at the table in an angry stalemate. Uncle John had the weed, Uncle Eddie had the papers, and neither one would budge. But I digress...

So the usual holiday plan was in place. I would go in the late morning and pick up UJ from his nursing home. He truly, truly hated it and could handle being out longer than my mother. Then I would come home and continue cooking everything for dinner with zero help from anyone. Jose would keep everything clean and everyone happy, but no one helped with the food, and Thanksgiving dinner is a motherfucker.

I had decided to brine the turkey

for the first time that year.

We left just after noon to get mom. Jose came along because the nursing home would no longer let the staff help me get her in the car and he was the only one strong enough to lift her. She also had gotten more accustomed to nursing home life than UJ, so she wanted to go back usually after a few hours. By the time everyone was there and settled, I was already stewing with mild rage and sadness from having to do so much by myself.

I set everything out and called everyone in for dinner. I took my first bite of turkey and the brining was a success. It was the most moist (sorry), delicious turkey I had ever made. I felt a brief moment of happiness and contentment. That was until Aunt spoke.

"This turkey is too moist."

I'm sorry, what? WHAT?!?

There is no such fucking thing. I went ape shit. Instead of backing off and realizing she pissed me off, she continued.

"Did you take your Prozac today?"

As if that didn't put me close enough to the edge, my mother then got concerned and wanted to know what that comment was all about.

"Kat, what?! You're on meds? Why?!"

Lovely. Fucking lovely.

It took every ounce of my patience and love for food to calm down and get through the rest of the meal.

Afterwards, I did all the transporting too. Mom, then UJ and Aunt last. Jose stayed back at the house with Aunt and UJ while my brother helped me get my mom back.

While I was gone, UJ was able to get stoned. What a wonderful idea. You see, high UJ assumes he can use the bathroom unassisted. Very, very untrue.

I came home to Jose cleaning my bathroom, which was now covered in Hep C tainted shit, all by himself.

Fanfuckingtastic.

Why not?

And then Emily came by just in time to take Uncle John back home.

She had already had a similar day with her dad, my uncle Eddie.

Thank god for Emily agreeing to walk him back inside the nursing home. He was in full on slow shuffle mode and it was raining. If I had had to take that 10 minute wet journey up a long ass ramp, I don't even know what I would've done.

So, now I've moved. I got a second floor apartment. On purpose. I just can't do all that again. Ever again.

Emily Alice

I was 5 when she was born. It was 1987. She's the only daughter of my Uncle Eddie, which (obviously) makes her my cousin, but she wasn't. She was my sister. She is my sister. She was my first best friend. She still is. One of my first memories of her is when my Aunt Sue took her out of the car and she had this giant bandage on her head. What in the fuck was this egg looking baby? I was so confused. Turns out she had to have some sort of cyst removed from her head or something, but I had been watching a shit ton of Mork and Mindy so I was convinced she was an alien.

(I'm still not 100% sold that she's not)

We used to get into some hilarious shit together when we were little. During most days, we were poorly supervised, if supervised at all. Almost all of our fuckery involved pranking Uncle John and Uncle Eddie. We would wait until Uncle Johnny passed out on the couch, sneak up behind him on the back of the couch then roll him off. We needed that couch, it was the centerpiece of most of our entertainment. It was the foundation of all blanket forts. It was our ship for escaping the hot lava. We would do this weird shit where we stood on the arms and say "I don't want to die, I don't want to die, but I have to die" and then collapse and bounce up from the cushions. Bizarre, I know, but we were some strange ass children that grew into some strange ass adults. She was around almost all of my childhood, except for the few years she lived in Florida. My Auntie Sue wanted to move south to see if maybe Uncle Eddie could get his shit together and clean up down there. Not so much...

I remember being so broken hearted when she left. I sat in my room, crying, while I recorded for her a custom cassette tape. It was the entire Lion King soundtrack, complete with sad depressing messages from me in between each song.

She's moved away and back a few times since then, but I handle it slightly better now. I love her so, so much. She is my sister. She is my Emily Alice.

Elephant Show

I remember when I was little, maybe 4. I had to be, because I hadn't started school yet. We would have to actually wait for a show to come on. There was no DVR. I'd watch Today's Special... a retrospectively terrifying show about mannequins that came alive at night after the store closed. Good ol' 80s TV. And right after, was my favorite, Sharon, Lois and Bram's Elephant show. I'd hurry up and get my mom, so she wouldn't miss the best part. (She didn't pay too much attention to the TV until Days of Our Lives came on)
She had to sit first, and then I'd sit on her lap. And then we sang together...

Skidamarink a dink a dink. [Put your right elbow in your left hand and wiggle your fingers.]
Skidamarink a doo. [Put your left elbow in your right hand and wiggle your fingers.]
I love you. [Point to yourself, hug yourself, and point to the other people in your group.]
Skidamarink a dink a dink.
Skidamarink a doo. I love you.I love you in the morning. [Make a big circle over your head with your arms, like the sun. Bend over to one side.]
And in the afternoon. [Stand up

straight with your arms above you.]
I love you in the evening. [Bend over to the other side.] And underneath the moon. [Make a small circle in front of your chest with your hands and move it over your head.]
Skidamarink a dink a dink.
Skidamarink a doo.
I love you.

She loved it just as much as I did.
Best time of the day.
I love you, mom

My First 10 Speed

I was in the 3rd grade, I think. Somewhere around 1990. We had received the materials to do our yearly school fundraiser and I was pumped. Those prizes were awesome. (Much more obtainable than they are now, but those were also the days of prizes in our cereal. I miss that shit.) My school had a separate initiative. Whoever sold the most products in the whole school would win a brand new 10 speed bike. Not that I didn't love my beautiful banana seat, but I was getting older. All my friends had 10 speeds and I wanted it bad. No fucking clue how to properly ride one, but I could figure that out later. I was all in. Back then you could actually go door to door to sell shit. Not sure if there were less pedophiles, or just less media coverage on the pedophilia. Either way it was legit and I was making sales like crazy. Between that and my mother and aunt bringing the book to work, I had made a killing. They had a special assembly and everything to announce the winner--me. I had done it. Risking abduction was totally worth it. That shit was mine! I waited and waited and the day finally came to take it home. I was so excited. I rode it as often as I could, trying every once in awhile to fuck with the gears and pretend I knew what I was doing. I was so happy.

I had that bike for 2 weeks before my uncle John, high on heroin, ran it over with his car.

Never did figure out those gears.

Iced Tea

I have always been a sucker for as long as I can remember. Is it because I try to always look for the good in people? Or because the wrong people see the good in me and use it to fuck with me? Probably a combination of both. I was generally the target of a mean girl, or six*. I always fell for their shit. "Kathy, if you give us a piece of your gum, we'll be your best friend." What kind of asshole falls for that? Me. They would befriend me when they weren't in their cunt cluster. It was safe to hang with me then. When they got together, that was another story. I lived in a nice neighborhood of nice houses and people with nicer bank accounts. Not us. We were broke. The house was left to my mother and aunt when my grandpa died. It was nice, at one time. Is again now. Just wasn't for the most part when I was living there. Shit luck for me.

One of the mean girls had a pool and it was hot as hell out. She invited me over for a swim. Part of me thought it was a set up. Part thought it was a shitty move even being friends with her. But all of me knew I needed to get my chubby ass in that fucking pool. There were only a few other girls there, and they weren't the dicks.

It was safe. For both of us. I went home in a great mood. I was cool, both figuratively and literally. Today was a new day. I walked in the door and remembered that we had ice cream. Perfect. I went marching in the kitchen, head high, grabbed a bowl and opened the freezer. We barely kept any food in there because my uncle would annihilate anything edible the second it came through the door. Another interesting thing my uncle would do is make iced tea. Tea is not very interesting, but his brewing method was.

He'd take a 2 quart Tupperware jug, fill it to the brim with water, pop in a handful of teabags and microwave for 15 minutes. Then he'd take that boiling shit show and put in the freezer until it was cold. The freezer had about 3 inches of ice build up along the bottom, but that instability didn't stop him. He had just made a fresh batch and popped it in there right before I walked in the door. Right beside the ice cream. I opened the freezer door and that shit came sliding down that ice mountain faster than I could process what was happening. Boiling hot tea had covered the whole front of my body, except my face. I looked away as it happened. My chest got it the worst. I screamed on the top of my lungs and ran around the house. I was completely in shock. Mom and Aunt knew just what to do. Have my freshly 2nd degree burned ass get in the cold shower.

That, to this day, was the worst pain I have felt in my life.

Emily said she was there too, but I couldn't even remember that. I do remember the EMTs peeling down my bathing suit and seeing the perfect V pattern the blisters had formed from the stitching on my bathing suit. Thankfully, it didn't leave me with any scars and it happened before my boobs came in. I couldn't swim in any pools for the rest of the summer, bitches or not. Probably saved me from joining their squad of shallow existence. Silver linings, I suppose.

*if you're reading this, and you're one of those girls, I forgive you. But also, fuck you. Forever. Xo.

The Night

Mom and Aunt spoiled me with so much love when I was growing up. I never doubted that I was loved. Unfortunately, they weren't very good at money management. Their spending habits caused my mother to have to constantly work at least two jobs, most of the time pulling doubles and sometimes triples just to make minimum credit card payments. My memories of her from my teenage years were mostly her shopping, working, smoking or sleeping. She barely ate regular meals and definitely didn't take care of herself. One night, while she was working, I went with Aunt to the mall. We were in the middle of eating when I got a call from the nursing home where she worked as a CNA. They told me my mother was throwing up and had passed out, so she was on her way to the ER. I was shook up, but not surprised she had gotten sick. I thought that was inevitable with her lifestyle. She must have passed out from not eating right, I was sure of it.

I arrived at the ER. I told them I was here to see Eileen and that she had just been brought in by ambulance. "Oh sure, right this way." They escorted Aunt and me to one of the triage rooms and smiled "she's right in here". I was ready to give her hell. She needed to start taking better care of herself and I wasn't gonna let up until she did.

The only problem is when I walked into that room, she wasn't sitting up waiting to be scolded by her 17 year old daughter. She was unconscious, her head was shaven, there were tubes coming out of it and someone was on her chest providing her oxygen.

Holy fucking shit.

No warning. Just a smile and she's right in here. That's what I got to prepare me. I short circuited. I remember the nurse asking Aunt "what's her problem?" Fucking cunt. Next thing I remember we were waiting for her to have surgery. She had a brain aneurysm. She was going in for a procedure called coiling, where they shoot tiny coils into the aneurysm to resume normal blood flow in the brain and stop the bleeding. She had a 5% chance of survival. Well, she made it.

The next year was pretty foggy in my memory. A few months in a coma, two or three more brain surgeries to correct infections, a tracheotomy, and having to watch my mother learn to walk again. She was able to walk for a little while, but that didn't last long. It's hard to stay motivated when your whole life changes in one night. So, now she lives in a nursing home. She's taken care of by CNAs, just like she was.

The last few weeks she's been in and out of the hospital again. She's currently in ICU recovering from a gallbladder removal. I struggle to go up there and see her like that. I walk through those doors, look at all those doctors, and it takes me right back to that night when I was 17 and thought she just needed something to eat.

Walking

Last year my great Aunt Mary passed away. She lived a good life. We can only hope to age as beautifully as she did. As it usually happens, we reconnected with family at her services that we hadn't seen in a while. I'm fortunate enough that my family, immediate and extended, is made up of truly wonderful and eclectic people. It was great to see them, even under the circumstances. There was discussion that we had to have a get together, in a better setting, very soon. My mom and Aunt were always very close to those cousins, so the idea of having a mini reunion was great. They ended up planning a cookout at Colt Park, a typical Rhode Island gathering spot. $2 a picnic table, can't beat it. They made a Facebook event to help everyone remember. People were posting old photos and memories in the event page. Who doesn't love seeing all that old shit? So my cousin puts up a video. Doesn't sound spectacular, but it was in the 90's. It wasn't like today where everyone records themselves eating sushi or getting wasted. There were unwanted giant camcorders in your face. Annoyed and unaware how much you would wish there were more. Anyways, he puts up this video of a cookout I had gone to in the mid '90s, I think. I knew I'd catch a glimpse of myself in wretched puberty and there would be a 50% chance I'd be wearing an Animaniacs shirt. I hit play with such optimism.

I saw Aunt walk by... then me... then her. My mother. And she was there and she was walking. She was her, Eileen. The one who walked me to the bus stop every morning in elementary school, and middle until I stopped her.
Why the fuck did I do that....The one who worked and worked and worked some more.

And she was walking.
She was ok.

It fucking punched me right in my heart. 17 years since I last saw her walk. Since she took care of me, not the other way around. She's still here, and I'm unbelievably grateful for that.

I'm very lucky, I know. But, man, 17 years and not one day has been easier than the last.

Woods

(originally shared online)

Always. I'm always daydreaming about running into the woods. Deep inside, where no one can find me until I'm ready to be found. Maybe inside a coyote den, pending they accept me as their own and don't try to eat me. That also works as a cop out to not have to build my own shelter. I'd stop by the bookstore on the way there and grab some sort of survival guide. Telling me what berries to avoid and how not to get a rash. Can't go to the library. Too many fines. Plus, they can use that to track me. I need to be untraceable. You think if I get in with the coyotes, the deer will reject me as a predator? Or accept me as the newest tenant? But, realistically, I can't. Even if I got the book and ditched the phone. Even if the coyotes thought I was cool. Because my daughter needs me. My daughters need me. I can't control the constant landslide of taco bell induced diarrhea that is my life. I need to make peace with that. I need to ride the brown waves and never fucking go overboard. I need to. For me. For them. So they have a constant. So they're not 34, sitting on a couch wondering where the fuck things went wrong... All the things.

Writing a story on a social media account, read by several people I don't know and won't ever know.

Telling all 104 of you that I want to run away and hide in the woods when all I really want is just one person to hug me and make me laugh until I'm not thinking about the cure for poison berries anymore.

Bob

A few days before Jose was supposed to leave, he went down to the town hall to fill out paperwork to give me guardianship over Angelina. He was always pretty terrible at paperwork, so he kind of just stood there dumbfounded. No idea where to even start. In walks Bob. He saw Jose was stressed, and listened to his story. He then sat with Jose for over an hour, helping him with all the legalities and paperwork. He told him my court date and wished him luck. Weeks later, I went to town court. A freshly single and stressed out mom, I was pretty overwhelmed myself. I had no idea what I was supposed to say. The plan was to just go with the flow. I saw Bob in the courtroom, but he was talking with one of his high profile clients, so I thought nothing of it. I had never met him. So they called my case, and he stepped forward.

"I'm here to represent her, your honor."

I was speechless. Not only was I a stranger, I hadn't paid this man a dime. He did all the talking for me, sealed the deal. That was that. I thanked him (over and over). He asked about Jose and wished him well.

He was just being a good guy, doing a good thing for no other reason than that's who he was. This is rare.

And, now he's gone.
I'm sure there are hundreds more stories of kind things he did for good people.
Rock on in the afterlife, Cool Moose. You were an awesome dude.

Truffle

It's 5:15pm. I worked all day and now I'm running errands so I haven't even made it home yet. I'm sitting here, in this place, waiting for my turn to pay bills and I'm hit with this sweet, sugary smell. I'm thinking to myself what is that smell? Is that someone's weird perfume? It's so strong! So my thoughts start drifting elsewhere but there it is again, assaulting my nostrils. Now it's driving me crazy because the scent is so familiar but I can't figure out. Then it hits me. I know what the smell is. I slowly reach into my scrub pocket and pull out what used to be a Lindt chocolate truffle. Holding the flat morsel with my chocolate covered hand, I look down and start geeking out to myself. I'm covered in it. It's on my undershirt. My pants. Everywhere. It's especially concentrated at the bottom of my scrub pocket, making me look like a giant 5 year child who hoards candy. How long have I been walking around like this?! As soon as the hilarity of all it wore off, I realize I'm becoming her. That woman. We all know her. There's one in every town. She's in her early 60s. She carries around a black patchwork leather pocketbook she got from the

Sunday paper coupons. It's filled with all the essentials:

A half a pack of Parliament lights.
Seven lipstick covered tissues.
A bus pass that expired 2 years prior.
A ripped envelope with a recent bank withdrawal in it.
A coupon for $1 off 7 cans of tuna.
2 peanut butter Nip candies, one partially unwrapped.

Her hair is 70% haphazard, 30% Aquanet. One shoe is untied, unless she's got the Velcro on today. In that case, one strap is always at a 45° angle and full of decades' worth of lint.

You don't pity her, but you can tell she's seen some shit and you want to be her friend just long enough to hear some of it.
Then you have to leave her alone. She's in the middle of her 27th round of Keno and she doesn't have time for your shit.
She doesn't become way this overnight. She didn't go to sleep one night an investment banker and wake up the next morning who she is today.

It took time. It started slowly. Scratch tickets and melted chocolates. This is how it all begins.

Landslide

I checked in at the front desk of the hospital and took a seat in the waiting area. Sometimes, in this fucked up ride that is my life, I have these moments of electric clarity and contemplation. They shake me out of the haze I exist in and redirect my attention to the now. Sometimes, it jerks me into noticing the magnitude of fuckery that I have to deal with personally. Those times I let myself feel it, then let it pass. Doesn't do anyone any good staying stuck in Bummerville. Sometimes, it's the opposite and I'm made aware of my surroundings--every tiny aspect. Smells, sounds, colors. It's hard to explain. Anyway, when I sat down, I had one of those moments. There was a mother and son there, also waiting, but they weren't sitting. They were rocking, back and forth while she sang 60s rock ballads to him. She kept in perfect step with each of his, back and forth. She had this exhausted Stevie Nicks vibe to her. Dressed for her era, and fantastically so, I might add. I looked at her eyes.

They were so, so tired, but so driven. In his lifetime, she must've sang him thousands of songs and rocked him thousands of times, but that's what made her child at peace. So she'll keep on it, singing a million more songs if it will help even a little.

When you're a mother, or parent, you are preset with the need to cure your child of any discomfort or heartbreak.

A kiss for a boo boo, a band aid for a bloody knee. But, sometimes you can't fix it. It's deep inside their brains and bodies where mommies and daddies can't reach. Nothing hurts a mother more, birth or otherwise, than knowing her child hurts and there's nothing she can do to stop it.

Sometimes, if you're unlucky enough, you experience this for a child and as a parent. And it's shitty. So we hug, we sing, we rock and we sacrifice.

If you ever have one of these moments like I did, and you see someone living this--doing their damnedest to keep someone at peace--take a moment and send them some love.

They need it.

Four for Four

Sitting at this fine dining establishment and enjoying my $6 lunch. This couple I recognize walk by with their $12 lunch. I know who they are because they have been sharing a struggle with me and they don't even know it. They also have a child in the mental health system, but that's all I know. I wonder where they're at in their struggle. Was their child's outburst a one-time thing? Is she cool now? Has she been medicated so heavily that no one even knows who she is anymore, including herself? Or are they still fighting? Working against, not with, a system set up only to benefit the insurance companies. Set up to dump 100 kids on the lap of 1 state employee who you've had no choice but to turn to for help. Help? Will their daughter be the one that gets that workers attention today? Tomorrow? Ever? Are they dealing with the courts? Judges and lawyers who are never, ever informed on what the fuck is going on, but have the power to decide their child's future?

If they are, is their daughter being coddled by the justice system? Being told essentially that she can fuck up to any extreme and show an immense lack of empathy and its ok? She has problems.

Her prefrontal cortex isn't fully developed. It's not her fault. Is she home? With them? Are they walking on eggshells, not knowing her next move?

Not knowing if today is going to be another day they have to spend 10 hours in the ER for psychiatric evaluations and then carry on with their day to day lives? Is she away? In the hospital? At a group home? Being someone she's not? Doing her best to become a shell of the person she has the potential to be? Have they given up? Are they still fighting? Are they here to escape all that?

To hold on to just 20 minutes of one meal without some level of unpredictable bullshit breaking out? Did they get ranch or honey mustard for their nuggets?

So many questions.

Starbucks

It was 8:45 am on a Saturday morning and I had already attempted to save a dog I watched get hit by a car and made a brief stop at the prison. Fuck, did I need a treat. So I went where all the cool kids go for pretentious refreshments, Starbucks. I didn't really have a game plan, which can really fuck your whole Starbucks experience up if the staff can't get on your level. Well, you on theirs, I guess. They are superior. No milk today. But caffeine. Yes. As much as I can get without drinking nut driven milk. I usually get this Strawberry Acai refresher, but I know they're judging me for saying Acai wrong. Maybe not that today. Oh, look. A new red drink. With berries. I think I'll get that. Shit. What size? What if it's gross? Fucking A, what's a god damn medium called again? Christ. It's my turn. Time to make some decisions. I decide to go with my classic. Grande Strawberry refresher. I leave the Acai out cause fuck them. I order Aliyah her usual frozen chocolate thing and went on my way. Waiting patiently in the sea of other caffeine zombies. Dude yells out some crazy shit and plops 2 red drinks on the counter. Now here's where I panic. I can't fucking remember what I ordered. Did I order that new berry shit or my usual? Fuck. Shit fuck. Some chick shimmies in and grabs the smaller one. She had on some cut up shirt that looked great on her. Me, I'd 100% look homeless. Not her. She pulled it off.

And she was confident that was her drink. No need for names or anxiety. Grabbed it and left. So that leaves just the one. It had to be mine. I grab it, pop a straw in and wait for Aliyah's. I get about 3 sips in when dude comes back with ANOTHER red drink.

And you know what? That one I'm CERTAIN is mine.

I walk over to the counter and make eye contact with the dude.

"Hey. So, I thought this was mine. But it's not. Annnd I drank some. So now what?"
I slid him my sin. He snatched that shit up like owed money. I fucked his whole shift up. He definitely was gonna talk shit about me to his family at dinner. So now I'm waiting for rage dude to make the new drink and here comes the owner of the soiled one. I feel the need to step in and tell him what's up. "Sir, I thought your drink was mine and I drank it and I'M SORRY!" Because, why not let my inability to control my volume and

awkwardness take charge here. Now everyone in the zombie pit is staring at me. Poor berry drink dude is so freaked out and thirsty. My bad, dude, if this reaches you.

"Grande double chocolaty chip Frappuccino!"

Finally, I can leave. But not without one more dash of Kathy saltiness. I march over, grab the cup and announce to everyone "THIS ONE IS DEFINITELY MINE!" and walk out.

So, yeah. That's why I can't ever go back to the Garden City Starbucks again.

White Rabbit

November 5, 2015

I was still holding the door open for Sunny when my phone rang. We hadn't even made it into the restaurant yet. It was Uncle John's nursing home, no doubt calling to tell me he fell again. He was always trying to do more than he should there. He hated being in that place. Never did adapt like most would have at that point. Always threatening to escape. He even was confined to the first floor because he once convinced a CNA to get him weed and a bowl. The cops agreed he needed to be more closely monitored.

The call was from a hospice representative. They had placed him on it about a year prior. Every time I went to see him he looked fine. Never any worse. They must be calling to tell me he's been removed from the list.

"There's been a change in John's status."

"So, he's better?"

"No. He's declined. You should come see him."

"Like dying? Right now?"

"Yes. You should come. Now, if you can."

Shit. It was happening. Right now. Besides Sunny, I had Aunt and both kids with me. We were all going to have to go, no time to bring anyone home. I called Emily on the way there so she could meet me. She happened to have just moved back from Oregon. One of those divine timing situations, I guess. Uncle John was a father figure to both of us. We were the closest he ever had to his own children. I needed her with me for this.

We managed to arrive at the nursing home at the same time. Emily and I went in first. We were greeted by a CNA on the walk up the ramp. "Are you John's family? I'm so sorry." That shit made this whole situation 100% real. "Talk to him. He can still hear you. Hearing is the last to go." This time he didn't look good like he usually did. He looked, well, like he was dying. I had never seen anyone this close to dying before. It's a pretty fucked up thing to witness. All these emotions slamming you all at once. If he can hear, he must be thinking. Jesus Christ, what is he thinking? About all the fucked up choices he made? Maybe just the good shit. Who knows? We casually said hi to him. Let him know we were there. Visiting UJ was always pretty awkward. He wasn't a man of many words, unless he was telling you a story. Like the time he took half a bag of peyote, climbed Mount Washington, then took the other half at the summit. Always some crazy ass shit.

We usually half listened to them, he repeated them so often. He always used to say "You know what they say… one pill makes you smaller.."

He'd go on and on.

Didn't realize until I was a teenager that it was actually a song.

Aunt was the first to make her move. Going in to say her final goodbyes. In true Aunt style, she went in really close to his ear and yelled "JOHNNY! JOHNNY! JOHNNY!"

Not in a 'this is it' way, but in a 'I'm going to keep hollering until he answers back' kind of way.

"Aunt! Jesus Christ! He's dying! Stop yelling at him!"

I couldn't let her shouting be the last thing he heard in his life. He would most definitely come back to haunt her ass.

But, what to say? I mean, it was awkward enough when he was conscious.

What the fuck do you even say to someone who is about to die? Good luck? Shit.

So, I decided I would save my words. It was no use. Instead, I chose to let him know that we had been listening to him all along. That we remembered his stories. Isn't that what we all want? Someone to listen to us. Not just hear us. Really fucking listen.

I sat beside him, pulled out my phone, and played 3 rounds of White Rabbit. So he would know that we were there. And we had listened.

I still want to believe his last thoughts weren't of the bad or of the good, but the hypnotic sound of Grace Slick chasing that White Rabbit one last time.

Cash

Uncle John was always paranoid "they" were gonna rob him. Always. Who "they" was changed over the years, but they were always there. First the nuns at Catholic school...then the cops. It stayed the cops for a while. Sometimes a shady character or two. But, even with that deep suspicion of those who didn't mean him well, he still shared what little he had. His weed, his stories, and even sometime his food. At the end, "they" was whoever surrounded him at the nursing home. He had 3 wallets AND a lock box to hide what little cash he had. All separate, so if he got robbed, he'd still be left with something. Maybe he was onto something. Don't dump all you've got in one spot. Spread it out. So if someone screws you, you're not left empty. Anyways, after he passed, we found this in his lock box. A photocopied wad of $20's that hospice made him so he could go out feeling secure.

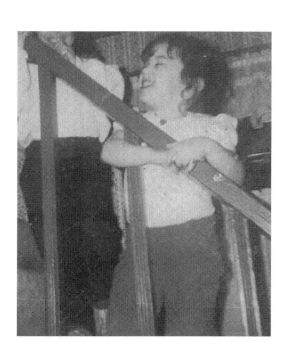

Made in the USA
Middletown, DE
20 June 2018